"*What is the definition of a good wine?*
It should start and end with a smile."
–William Sokolin

The grapes of Montemaggiore

Copyright Information

Wineries Beyond Napa Valley: **Dry Creek & Alexander Valley**
An Insider's Tasting Guide to the Hidden Gems of the region

ISBN-10: 0-615-23107-1
ISBN-13: 978-0-615-23107-5

For more information, please contact the publisher at
Beyond Napa Valley, 742 Via Casitas, Greenbrae, CA 94904
(415) 408-0071 | haydn@beyondnapavalley.com
www.beyondnapavalley.com

Gloria in excelsis Deo

Dedication

This book is dedicated to my Dad, Jeff, my sister, Kayln, and to my Grandparents, Glen and Ev Blackley. Somehow, through all my wacky and crazy endeavors, you guys still love me. I truly am a cheeseburger in paradise.

In Memory

The book is also dedicated in memory of my Mom, Karen, who died of breast cancer at the age of 36. She probably did more for me in the 11 years I knew her than I'll ever know.

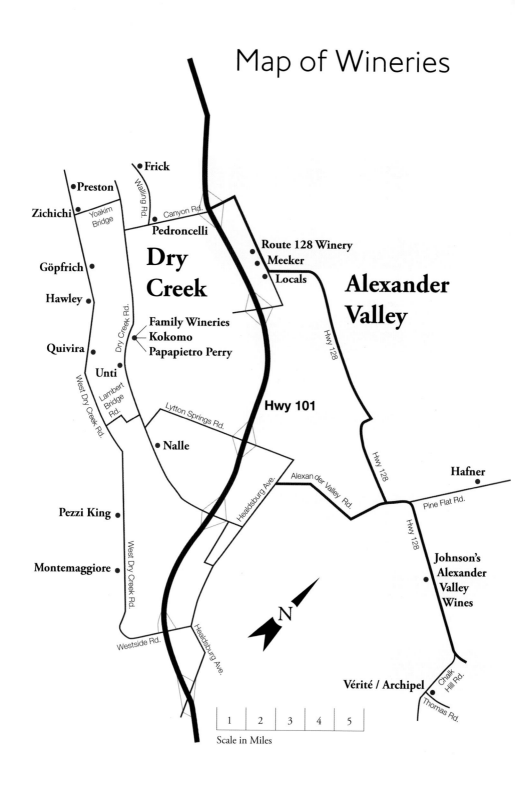

Map of Wineries

Frick

Preston

Zichichi

Yoakim Bridge

Walling Rd.

Canyon Rd.

Pedroncelli

Dry Creek

Göpfrich

Route 128 Winery

Meeker

Locals

Alexander Valley

Hawley

Dry Creek Rd.

Family Wineries
Kokomo
Papapietro Perry

Quivira

Unti

West Dry Creek Rd.

Lambert Bridge Rd.

Lytton Springs Rd.

Hwy 128

Hwy 101

Nalle

Healdsburg Ave.

Alexander Valley Rd.

Hafner

Hwy 128

Pezzi King

Pine Flat Rd.

West Dry Creek Rd.

Hwy 128

Johnson's
Alexander
Valley
Wines

Montemaggiore

N

Healdsburg Ave.

Westside Rd.

Vérité / Archipel

Chalk Hill Rd.

Thomas Rd.

| 1 | 2 | 3 | 4 | 5 |

Scale in Miles

Table of Contents

Special Thanks

No man is truly an island. Yes, I did find myself sitting at my kitchen table, in the middle seat of an airplane, or at some coffee shop downtown with only my laptop for company, talking to myself and sitting in splendid isolation. In reality, however, this book would have never left the "you're crazy" stage without a handful of people.

There are many people who helped make this book possible, yet if I were to include all of them in this section, half the book would be just this chapter. So do forgive me in advance if I left your name off.

First, a huge hug and big thank you to Jennifer Burden at Quivira. She was among the first to hear about this hair-brained idea of mine and was very influential along the way. She was also among the first to read the copy (that's design lingo for text) and I valued her opinion. Every time I sent her a chapter, I crossed my fingers in the hope she would give it a thumbs up.

To all the wine makers, owners and contact people at the 20 wineries I visited, I say thank you: Doug Nalle, Julie Pedroncelli, Steve Zichichi, Doug Hafner, Ray Gopfrich, Vince Ciolino, Steven Canter, Shirley Buchignani, Jackie Patrick.

Dave Barr, Helen Sherritt, Joan and David Waisbein. They listened patiently to my persistent auditory descriptions about the wine I was tasting and for accommodating me with guest rooms and couches while I spent time in the wine country.

A special thank you to Joan Tabb Waisbein, a wonderful marketing friend and colleague, who continually encouraged me to bring more of my personal vision and knowledge to the book.

Linda Anderson, my business coach, for all her help and encouragement. Writing a book is a little like driving a car cross country and, after driving through the emptiness of Nevada, you realize you're only 15 percent of the way there, and you're already tired. Linda's kinda like the XM radio for my life.

She keeps me tuned in and on track. And she's probably relieved that I actually finished a book after countless stops and starts on others.

Samantha Bronson, my editor for this book. This book couldn't have happened with out her expertise. She was there from the very beginning and will hopefully be there in the future as I continue to write. Thank you, Samantha!

Lastly, I need to give praise to two family members without whom this book would still be sitting in my head instead of your hands. The first, my Grandfather, Glen Blackley, one of the smartest businessmen out there and a great family guy. I often say, "If only I had listened to him sooner," from his invaluable lessons in business and in life.

And I thank my Dad, Jeff Adams, who taught me how to fish instead of buying the fish for me. He never complained if I reeled in an old boot out of the ocean instead of a tuna. I guess he figured I could always toss my line back in and give it another try. His insightfulness and entrepreneurship was invaluable and essential to this book. He's just the best father one could ever ask for.

Finally, to all of my readers out there. Thank you for support. I hope you have found some wonderful places to wine taste— beyond Napa Valley.

"Now there's only two things in life, but I forget what they are."
– John Hiatt

Foreword

First and foremost… BUY THIS BOOK! If you are truly looking for the "hidden gems" as Haydn calls them, in the Dry Creek and Alexander Valley's, then this is the book for you. It has been a joy helping Haydn with recommendations for some of the most unique, family owned wineries in Northern Sonoma County. This book is not stuffy, pretentious or intimidating… it is pure fun, which is how wine tasting should be. Haydn brings a wonderful sense of humor and wealth of knowledge to this book so all wine lovers, from beginners to advanced, will appreciate his approach to wine tasting. So if you want to really explore and get an insider's view of the Dry Creek and Alexander Valley's, purchase this book and make sure to have it handy as you drive through some of the most beautiful country in California.

We look forward to seeing you!

Cheers,

Jennifer Burden

Direct Sales Manager
Quivira Vineyards & Winery

Introduction

I've had my fair share of fruit-bomb Merlots and over-oaked Chardonnays. The steep tasting prices, the crowded tasting rooms, the over-the-top, "you really need to buy this one," sales pitches the wineries gave me. The allure of wine tasting in Napa Valley quickly waned for me.

When I first started wine tasting in Northern California, I assumed that Napa was the place to go tasting. All the big boys were there—Beringer, Sutter Home, Mondavi. But the more time I spent in Napa, the less excited I became about that region, so I went exploring.

I stumbled upon two relatively quiet regions: Dry Creek and Alexander Valley. I grabbed a wine map featuring these two regions and randomly chose a few wineries. I quickly loaded my car with the necessary wine tasting equipment: cooler, water, crackers (see tasting tips for more information), topped off my fuel tank and away I went up Highway 101 to discover this new world for myself.

Wow! It was as if I had landed in another country. The tasting fees were reasonable, the wineries were charming and the overall atmosphere was serene. The personalized attention I received was a welcomed treat. I began to try more and more of the wineries of the region. I was having a blast.

But I wanted a book that went deeper into the wineries, since there is so much more to wine tasting than the wine itself. I wanted to know what the tasting room was like, whether reservations were needed or if I could just stroll right in. I was curious about the overall characteristics of the winery. I wanted information on the wineries that went beyond wine ratings and national magazine reviews.

And so the idea for this book was born. I slowly began creating a "hidden gems" list of wineries I wanted people to try. To me, a hidden gem is a winery that is off the radar to most wine tasters. Some of these wineries are right out in the open, yet remain relatively undiscovered; others are tucked high in the hills with only an address on a mailbox to mark their location. Each one has something extra, from a "mom and pop" feel to a bit of humor and playfulness.

Combining the two wine regions, Dry Creek and Alexander Valley, I built my list of 20 wineries that I consider hidden gems. I'm honored to present them to you.

Cheers,
Haydn

Tips & Tasting Techniques

Below are a few tips to make your next wine tasting trip more enjoyable. It is my hope that you make the most out of your wine tasting experience and that your outing is both exciting and safe.

The cooler (no ice)

I've learned this tip the hard way by overcooking wine in the car. It was a modest winter day, sunny and probably in the low 60s. A storm had recently passed and I was enjoying the crisp air that preceded the rain. Stopping at some new places, I picked up a few reds and put them in the back seat of the car. After four hours of sitting in direct sunlight, with the car getting up in temperature, I basically slow-baked my bottles, leaving them more to remember than to savor.

These days I travel with a cooler in my trunk. The reason for bringing the cooler is not to chill the wine, but rather to maintain a consistent temperature and to keep the wine out of the sunlight. A reasonable day spent tasting can easily last four hours or longer. I'm not one to bank on the weather not overtaking my wine.

If the weather is exceptionally warm, I might place a blue ice pack into the cooler to keep it a bit colder. Remember that wines like underground caves where there is little temperature fluctuation and no sunlight. Your car is a foreign land, so at least provide a bit of safety to the bottles by keeping them in a cooler environment.

Lastly, if you do bring a wine cooler, bring one that is large enough to fill with a case of wine. You might not buy an entire dozen, but if you are with friends, it's easy to quickly load up on wine. Having to decide which bottle is saved and which bottle is destined to be banished to the sun and hot car is not a decision I would want to make.

Water and crackers

If you plan to stop at more than one winery, it's a good idea to bring along a water bottle or two. It's easy to get caught up in the wine tasting process and lose track of how many small sips you've taken. While they might look small and appear even smaller in big glasses when you try upwards of five to seven different varietals at a single stop, those little sips can catch up to you, especially if you are trying wines with 15-16% alcohol content. By having some water bottles in the car, you can hydrate yourself and not feel impaired quickly. After all, the whole goal here is to taste the wine and not become intoxicated too quickly.

Crackers help by getting a little food in your stomach. Don't choose the ones that contain onions, garlic, roasted pepper or anything close to something spicy. The blander the better. Crackers also help to neutralize your palette, much like ginger does for sushi.

Spitting

If you are the designated driver, someone who wants to have a strong sense of taste and smell at the end of the day or simply want to stay fairly sober, I'd highly recommend spitting. This is probably the only time, aside from baseball, where spitting is appropriate. If you do decide to spit, and I know this may sound obvious, be aware of where the spit buckets are and situate yourself somewhat near them. Some wineries will provide you with a smaller spit bucket for you to use, so it's not necessary to use the main bucket. While the concept may be visually repulsive, it's the only way to effectively try a good assortment of wine and not become intoxicated.

A Wine Map

Bring a wine map with you. Someone you meet along the way might recommend a new winery and having a map beats attempting to draw one on a napkin.

Don't Forget to smell

One of the most important attributes of a wine is its smell, or bouquet. Many people quickly sniff and drink, leaving little time to let the smell envelope their senses. Stick your nose all the way in the glass if you have to! There is a reason why glasses have large openings. It's both for the wine to expel some aromas and for you to get that nose all the way in there.

Certain wines need time to breathe. A wine that has just been opened will display different characteristics than the same bottle that was opened an hour ago. If you cannot distinguish any characteristics in the bouquet of the wine, give it a good swirl in your glass (though do be careful to not spill any). The wine will mix with the oxygen, setting off a whirlwind of aromas.

The common description for how the wine smells is its "nose." Frequently, you will read something like, "The nose on this wine has a fruit-forward complex with subtle hints of vanilla." It's just a guide, so don't flog yourself if the wine you are sniffing is said to smell like honey and you smell a Vicks® cough drop. All our senses are built upon prior experiences, and your olfactory senses might pick up something different than what is written. Trust your nose and use it constantly while tasting.

Sometimes the nose can be so delightful that you will delay sipping, just to languish in the beautiful aromas of the wine. If that is the case, keep smelling. I've been to wineries where I almost want to forego drinking a wine because the bouquet is so beautiful. I eventually come to my senses.

Taste, taste, taste
and you pick out what you taste

Cherries wrapped in bacon. Wet dirt and mushrooms. A dirty old attic. Roasted strawberries. These are a few of the descriptions I've heard other people give about wine. And the fun part is, there is no wrong description.

Some wineries don't give you tasting notes, allowing you complete control over what you smell and taste. Have fun and get creative. You never know, the next wine could end up smelling like your old little league baseball glove or wet dirt.

Don't be afraid to not like the wine

If you don't like the wine, stop drinking it and pour it out. Trust me. You won't hurt the feeling of the person pouring. With wineries numbering in the hundreds and each winery producing a wide array of wines, chances are good you won't like every wine.

Avoid spicy foods

Don't load up your huevos rancheros with the habanero salsa the morning of your wine tasting. You'll fry your taste buds from anything spicy and leave your mouth unable to distinguish characteristics of the wine. As a fan of spicy foods, I have to be especially aware of what I'm eating prior to tasting. Eventually your senses will return after eating spicy foods, but not for a matter of hours, so be careful.

What not to wear

Ladies and Gentlemen, please keep your perfumes and colognes at home. I know, you might think you smell great, but remember wine tasters would rather smell the wine, not you.

You'll not only do yourself a disservice in dousing yourself in Chanel No. 5, but the smells will permeate the tasting room and nullify everyone's senses faster than a chile relleno. If you think walking into a tasting room while intoxicated is uncool, wait until you walk in smelling like you bathed in Old Spice.

Mints, coffee and brushing your teeth

Along with spicy foods, mints will also do the trick in killing your taste buds. Between tasting rooms, you might think to yourself that your breath could really do without the prior wine's aftertaste and reach for that easy-to-get-to tin of Altoids®. Resist the temptation, otherwise your next sip of Sauvignon Blanc might contain hints of mint in it.

Coffee is also best avoided nearer to tasting. I admit, I can't start my day without a strong brewed cup of coffee. However, if you need to jolt your day by the ol' cup-o-joe, drink it as early as possible. Give your taste buds time to regroup and energized for tasting. This also goes for after-lunch espressos and cappuccinos. Feel free post-tasting to indulge in a latte or mocha, but only after you've finished tasting for the day.

While we're talking about early morning routines, think about when you brush your teeth. The minty-fresh feeling you get from your toothpaste, floss and mouthwash do the same thing as if you popped a mint. I recommend that the last thing you do after you brush your teeth is rinse your mouth with water so that not only are your teeth sparkling, but your palette is as fresh as possible as well.

Let's go tasting!

Now that we have our bases covered, let's go wine tasting.

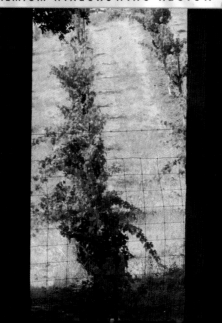

NOW ENTERING

DRY CREEK VALLEY

SONOMA COUNTY

PREMIUM WINEGROWING REGION

Dry Creek

You're in Zin County. Nowhere else in California will you find such an extensive collection of Zinfandels (no, not white Zin) in one region. Dry Creek is one of the smallest AVAs (wine region or American Viticultural Area) at only two miles across and sixteen miles long. However, you're bound to find more spice and pepper than in most home kitchens, in this valley.

Dry Creek is beautiful, a hidden gem nestled between two rows of mountains. It is a throw back to the day when Sunday drives were leisurely, the general store was the focal point of the town, and where owners & wine makers still poured the wine for you.

Dry Creek's climate is similar to the Bordeaux region of France. Fog might creep in during the morning hours, but the sun quickly takes over and jumps the mercury to the mid 80s during the growing season. Over the summertime, temperatures can breach the one-hundred degree mark.

If Zinfandel was the valley's staple wine for the red category, Sauvignon Blanc would be the staple for the white. Very few whites are produced, due to the climate of the region. You're also bound to find some wines you might have never heard of, including the Grenache, Sangiovese and Viognier.

I've selected fourteen wineries that I felt worthy of the term hidden gem for this region. Some are by appointment, hidden away from plain sight. Others are right on the main street of the valley. However, each one of the wineries has a unique characteristic that I've highlighted in the following chapters.

Drive safely. Welcome to Dry Creek.

Frick

Location
23072 Walling Road
Geyserville, CA

Phone
(707) 857-1980

Hours of Operation
Weekends 12:00–4:30

Tasting Fee
$5

One of the reasons I enjoy wine tasting in Dry Creek is the personable feel many of the wineries impart. Oftentimes, the winemaker or a family member of the winery is pouring their own creation for you. And it is those times when you get to taste the wine right in front of the very person who put their heart and soul into the delightful liquid that the most information and education can be found. Such is the case with Frick Winery.

Frick Winery sits up on the northeast side of Dry Creek. Watch out for Walling Road because it's easy to get captivated with Pedroncelli, sitting on the corner of Walling and Canyon and zoom right passed the turnoff. Yours truly did it once, even knowing where the road was. About a mile up the road is the tasting room. A dark-colored sign with the winery's name is nailed to a large evergreen tree. Once you see the sign, bear to the right and you'll find a parking lot for about a dozen cars. To further drive home the point that you are at Frick Winery, there is just to the north what I like to call, the "Leaning water tower of Frick." It's a wooden water tower, leaning a few degrees toward the tasting room.

The tasting room is marked by a large red door. It's basically a house turned tasting room. A white picket fence further complements the decor outside. A sign, "BEWARE! Extremely friendly dog," can be found right next to the entrance. That statement comes true as you walk inside and find Lucia begging for a great pet and scratch.

The tasting room is eclectic. Various cases of wine, modern artwork drawn by the owner's late wife, a periodic table of wine (that is more important than one might think) an old dresser, vintage wine advertising and other sellable materials dart the walls. Somehow all the diverse pieces seem to work harmoniously.

The types of wines Frick makes are about as diverse as the decor. Looking at the list of wines, I had to admit that a few of them I had yet to try or even really know about outside of Wikipedia. The three more unusual wines at Frick would have to be the Grenache Blanc, the Cinsaut (pronounced sin-so) and the Carignane. To learn more about these wines than you can get from drinking them, Bill Frick provides photos of the grapes, letting you get a better understanding of their makeup and character.

The visual of the grape and taste of the wine not enough for you? In that case, Bill's tasting notes come complete with pronunciation guide (which I failed to note and called the Cinsaut, phonetically spelled, a Cinsalt). That is very helpful when talking about the individual wines you're drinking. In addition, a light description of the wine and suggested food pairings were listed on the sheet. While descriptions of the taste of the wine are as common at wineries as Chardonnays are on the menus of restaurants, the food pairings are usually either buried on the wineries' web sites or not even written down at all. I was delighted to take the sheet home with me to help pair the Merlot I bought with an appropriate dish. Foodies will be delighted, I'm sure. (If you forget to take home a tasting sheet, all of the food pairings are listed on Frick's web site.)

The one wine missing from the list was the ever popular Dry Creek standard, Zinfandel. At first I was surprised to see the region's most prized grape missing from the list, but as I traveled through Frick's diverse collection, I forgot all about it and my questionable nature quickly turned to curiosity.

Another wine that was surprising was the Merlot. Normally a berry blast, this wine was deep in flavor, earthy and spicy. It was a huge difference compared to most of the Merlots out there. If you are dying for a Zin to hit your lips, close your eyes and try the Merlot. I think you'll be pleasantly surprised and satisfied.

A nominal $5 fee applies to tasting the wine and is probably refunded upon bottle purchase. The wines' prices range from $19 for the Cinsaut rosé, to $27 for the Viognier and Grenache Blanc. The price for both the tasting and the more unique grapes poured here make the prices more than reasonable.

For a bit of a detour from the normal grapes (Cabernet Sauvignon, Chardonnay and Zinfandel) and a traditional tasting room experience, check out Frick Winery (no, Frack's winery is not next door). The eclectic mix of decor, wine and artwork all work together for this winery.

Preston

Location
9282 West Dry Creek Road
Healdsburg, CA

Phone
(707) 433-3372

Hours of Operation
Daily approx. 11:00–4:30

Tasting Fee
$5
Waived with purchase

At first glance, you might mistake Preston for a farm. You'd be right. Well, sort of. While winemaking is the dominating force that drives this company, you're greeted by fresh vegetables for sale along the porch before even setting foot inside of the tasting room. Both the vegetables and the wine here are produced organically. A big thumbs up in my book.

Preston is located at the northern end of West Dry Creek Road. The only other one that is farther along the road is Bella, at the very end. Be sure to keep your eyes out for the turnoff for Preston, as it is a bit hard to see. I admit that I even had a tad bit of difficulty finding the location. Wine maps are not always perfect in putting the dot in the right spot.

Upon entering the grounds of Preston, there are some ground rules laid out on a large sign. For starters, no groups over eight. If you are traveling in a small group, say up to four, a larger group hogs the attention of the winery staff and can be a drag on the overall tasting experience of a particular winery. If you are traveling with a larger group (say over eight), now's the time to cross off Preston as a place to visit.

Preston continues with more house rules. They ask that you only consume their wine outside on the patio and not that of other producers. I don't want to know the consequences of bringing a Napa Valley wine or any Charles Shaw varietal onto the property. While it seems pretty obvious, visitors opening up wines from other vintners happens more times than wineries wish it would. A few more rules are listed on the sign, but those two are the main points the winery wishes to make.

Preston is a perfect place to have a picnic. The grounds and tasting room are about a quarter mile off of the road, so you will have little to no car noise, with the exception of the cars entering and exiting the parking lot. Well-manicured bushes and flowers, even-colored green lawn and an array of tables and chairs make the outside grounds that much more inviting. The sounds of a fountain just add the cherry to the top of the sundae. A cat can be seen roving the grounds, a departure from the usual dogs roving varying Dry Creek wineries. Cat lovers will appreciate it.

A country motif is clearly evident here, from the white chipped columns outlining the porch area, the metal watering can and fresh vegetables dotting the outside area. If it weren't for the fact that I was going for the original purpose of wine tasting, I would think this is more of a farmers market or a rustic country house than a winery and tasting room.

However, once inside (and don't let the cat in, according to the sign posted on the door), the ideals of a farmers market vanish and the standard sights of a tasting room become clearly apparent. A good collection of wine accessories dot the immediate area in front of the tasting bar. Towards the back are olive oils and breads. A collection of wearable goods, bearing the wineries' name, can also be found throughout the tasting room.

The actual space for tasting wine is smaller than other tasting rooms. While I haven't been here on a busy day, I would venture to say that the tasting room could get quite crowded. So if you do plan to go, I suggest Preston be the first winery to hit in the morning or one of the last to go to in the afternoon.

All of the wines are made from organically grown grapes, which means no pesticides or chemicals have been used in the winemaking process. I tend to gravitate more to the organic wineries. Maybe it is me, but I seem to be able to taste a certain freshness in the wines. I have done a blind taste test with organic wines, so I know it is not from just thinking about the organic aspect.

Upon approaching the tasting bar, you have the choice of four wines for $5. If you buy a bottle, the tasting fee is waived. Preston's winemaking is much in line with the Rhone style, so you're in for some deeper/smokier wines. If it is just you and one other person and you don't mind sharing a glass (to all the germophobes out there, remember we're drinking alcohol here, not licking an empty coke bottle), this would be a good place for each of you to pick separate wines and take a little sampling of each.

A great aspect of Preston's wines is that they started out fruit driven and gradually began to darken in color and lost the fruit all together at the end and turned into, as one customer said, "wine that tastes like cherries wrapped in bacon."

This is a great place to try some new wines you might have previously overlooked or didn't try in the past. While they do make two Dry Creek standards—Sauvignon Blanc and Zinfandel—Preston also has some you might have never tried, such as a Barbera, a Petite Sirah and a Marsanne.

Also, if your plans call for heading up to Dry Creek for the weekend, I suggest stopping into Preston on Sunday as this is the day you are able to taste the jug wine. My initial reaction to jug wine is the same reaction a sommelier would have if you asked him or her to pick out wine from Wal-Mart to stock at a restaurant. However, I did want to see and taste this jug wine for myself. It's funny, but while this wine was not my clear favorite, I'd say it ranks in my top five at Preston. It was just an easy going, spaghetti-served-for-dinner kind of wine. Their "Guadagni Red" comes in a three-liter jug and is a great bang for the buck at $32. If you bring back the jug, they take $2 off of the price.

Overall, Preston is rustic and country-inspired. The ambience and décor speak highly to a farm style of living. The bottle design, wood flooring and simple life further adds to that lifestyle. And while all the signs point to country living, with cornbread and gravy probably being cooked in the next room, one cannot get around that the wine is good and fresh. The staff is friendly, knowledgeable and will make you feel welcome from the moment you open the door. As long as you don't let the cat in.

FAMILY VINEYARD

OPEN

8

Zichichi

Location
8626 West Dry Creek Rd.
Healdsburg, CA

Phone
(707) 433-4410

Hours of Operation
Daily approx. 11:00–5:00

Tasting Fee
None

It's quite easy to find Zichichi Vineyards but a bit more troublesome to pronounce. Zichichi (Zee-Kee-Kee) Vineyards was founded by former Louisiana doctor, Steve Zichichi. And while his roots in winemaking are not even a decade old, he did pick some of the more wiser vines in the valley. If you are going on the old adage that with age, comes wisdom, then his grapes are some of the wisest at nearly eighty years old.

Following the aftermath of hurricane Katrina, Steve Zichichi decided to move west and establish himself in the wine world. He couldn't have chosen a more picturesque location in Dry Creek. Sitting about a hundred feet off of the valley floor, his tasting room has unparalleled views of the valley, both north and south. The tasting room smells fresh, with light hints of pine and cedar dancing around. It's quite apparent the room is only a few years old; the "new tasting room" smell is still lingering.

On the patio, a few chairs and tables are arranged to maximize the beautiful views. A few ceiling fans hang from the tops of the wood slats that provide a bit of shade to relaxing patrons. The tasting room and outside deck felt very homely. I stood out there for a few minutes, breathing in the crisp air that was quickly warming from the sun's rays. The valley was quiet and the only sound I heard was Jimmy Buffett coming from the two speakers overhead. I gave a quick chuckle realizing that I was sitting at a winery all the while listening to a man who has done more to boost the tequila industry than probably any other person out there (for the record, I'm a parrot head). The music further added to the homely feel that this winery brought.

The stone fireplace, the smaller square footage and the fresh flowers (I think they were a type of gardenia) all make you feel as though you are stepping into somebody's home rather than a business. With Steve conducting the pouring, that just sealed the deal. The tasting room is intimate. Different apparel items dot the wood tables and other trinkets and treasures can be found around the room.

At the time I was there, only one wine was currently bottled but you were able to taste three wines. That's because he does something that usually is reserved for once a year festivities—barrel tasting. While most wineries hold exclusive parties and charge fair prices to get a small glimpse, or rather taste, of the in-process wine, Steve opens his barrels year-round for anyone who walks in the door.

The tasting begins at the well-manicured tasting bar with the solo old-vine Zinfandel. Following that, you're walked into the cellar and given the chance to barrel taste. Now, tasting wine before it has been properly barrel-aged is kind of like predicting the college major of a 15-year-old. Looking at family history, interests and activities, you have a pretty good idea of where he or she is going, but there is still a chance that he or she could still run off and join the circus. With barrel tasting, it's the same thing. And Steve is a good shepherd, instructing patrons on what to look for in the wine. Younger wines pre-bottled have smells and tastes that are subdued, so spend a bit more time swirling, swishing and smelling (note, no spit bucket present so no spitting unless you're willing to use the drain on the floor).

Steve is very receptive to any questions you might have about buying before bottling. And besides, tasting straight from the barrel is quite fun. Where else can you easily use the word bung hole and not offend anyone?

Pedroncelli

Location
1220 Canyon Rd.
Geyserville, CA

Phone
(800) 836-3894

Hours of Operation
Daily 10:00–4:30

Tasting Fee
None

The story of the Pedroncelli Family Winery starts with an ending. The year was 1934 and it marked the end of prohibition. For five years, John Pedroncelli Sr. was limited to selling grapes to homeowners in the neighborhood in order to keep the vineyard going. Now that prohibition was only a memory, John turned his attention to wine making and from then on, Pedroncelli has never looked back.

And after eighty years of being in the business, the Pedroncelli family is still tending to the grapes, blending the wines, and, at times, even pouring them in the tasting room. Three generations have been working in this winery and their commitment to quality wines and a great feeling comes out. A small block of 100-year-old Zinfandel still sits on the property today, as testament to commitment. You can also see the original bonded winery number on the side of the barn, #113, right next to the tasting room. This might seem inconsequential until you realize that there are over 2,700 wineries in California today and the numbers are given out in sequential order.

In the tasting room, you immediately feel welcome. The room is open and inviting. Different bottles of wine are placed along the varying walls with Christmas lights turning on and off around the upright bottles. The wood columns are natural, they are unpolished but still evoke a warm feeling. The bar consists of two tasting areas, separated by a large wooden beam where the two meet at a 90 degree angle. The actual bar is wood, smoothed and polished so your glass can be easily swirled.

The outside of the tasting room is as rustic-looking as the inside. The winery sits all by itself out on canyon road, so if you are looking to maximize your wine-tasting-per-mile experience, you'll have to drive a little bit to get there. The winery is located on the northern end of the Dry Creek Valley. While it is easy to find, it is a bit more of drive than the wineries on the southern end, such as Wilson. The shape of the region is long and narrow. If you do decide to give Pedroncelli a try, give yourself a little extra time to get there. There is adequate parking along with a slew of picnic tables out on the patio along with a bocce ball court.

Another great reason to visit Pedroncelli is that you can look outside and see where some of the grapes are being grown for the wines. All of Pedroncelli's grapes are grown within 10 miles of where the grapes are harvested and the wines are made. While other winery-owned vineyards might be scattered around the valley, or even in other AVAs, Pedroncelli's are literally within walking distance.

Pedroncelli prides itself on "staying the course." From year to year, the wines remain consistent. For someone who finds and loves a great wine, this is a blessing. Other wineries will vary the style of winemaking for a particular wine from year to year. What that means is that an '04 merlot, for example, might be beautiful and ripe (remember, Merlots usually have a good berry flavor) and it just hits your taste buds perfectly. Then the following year, the winemaker might decide to add some Cabernet Sauvignon in it and the '05 totally goes against what you like. With Pedroncelli, you're not going to get that. While slight variations are bound to happen, you'll find a consistency in the wine making.

At the time of this writing, Pedroncelli did not charge for tastings. It's a rare but welcome sight, with most wineries in the region charging around $5 and Napa commanding $10 to $15. The pourers, some of whom are Pedroncellis, are very knowledgeable about the slew of wines they offer. And with nearly a dozen varietals to choose from, that is no small task. The wines range from the two white wines, Sauvignon Blanc and Chardonnay, to the Dry Creek-grown port, derived from four different port grapes. At a tasting, you are given the choice of six tastes. Choosing six out of a dozen wines is not done easily.

Their wines are styled to be "food wines." Pedroncelli states, "They are approachable wines, like a best friend who joins you for an informal, easy-going evening." I agree. In tasting them, I found that a smile kept coming over my face. There are wines that are tougher and more complex to figure out than the Sunday New York Times crossword puzzle. And while I enjoy those at times, my mind sometimes focuses on figuring out the subtle nuances of a mid-palette, aftertaste and other areas of the wine. With these wines, I could see sitting down with an old friend and simply enjoying the pleasant palette and smooth and balanced finish with each of the wines. While some wines did show a bit more tannins than I would be comfortable with, a lay down in the cellar for a year or so would solve the problem. However, with nearly all of them, I'd say they are fine to drink now.

The prices for Pedroncelli's wines are very affordable. Even the beloved Pinot Noir, after taking a spike from a certain Hollywood movie (*Sideways*), is in the $20s. With good Pinots commanding at least $60 and up these days, it is great to see a Pinot priced in an affordable price range. And pinot grapes are not the most cooperative grape, so generally more time and energy goes into the care of the Pinot Noir. On Pedroncelli's price list, nothing went over $25. Keep in mind that wine prices do fluctuate, so be aware that the prices here are from the time of my writing, not necessarily the latest price.

Göpfrich

Location
7564 West Dry Creek Rd.
Healdsburg, CA

Phone
(707) 433-1645

Hours of Operation
Weekends 11:00–4:00
By appointment

Tasting Fee
None

When wine tasting in Dry Creek, you'll find that Rieslings are more readily found in local supermarkets than on tasting room counters. The climate is warm and Zin friendly and not well-suited for this Germanic grape. The abundant white that is not afraid to show its face around these parts is the Sauvignon Blanc, but the Riesling has found a place to shine in Dry Creek. Welcome to Gopfrich Winery.

Having not lost ties to the German wine world, Ray Gopfrich offers his patrons the chance to taste white wine imported from Germany along with traditional Dry Creek standards, Zinfandel, Cabernet Sauvignon, Syrah, and a rosé made from Zinfandel grapes.

Gopfrich is open on the weekends only and by appointment. It's not difficult to find the winery, but it is a bit of a drive on West Dry Creek Road to reach the property, so do give yourself a little extra time to get there. With the narrowness of West Dry Creek Road and the abundance of road bikers, chances are good you'll be traveling below the speed limit to get here.

The tasting room is very cozy. A large sign promoting the Umlaut, the name of Gopfrich's wine club, can be seen immediately upon entering, along with a large central table. Around the room are illustrations of animals with the Umlaut, an "O" for a mouth and the two dots for either the nose or eyes. As an artist, I was captivated by the many different animals drawn. Along with the artwork, various awards and medals were displayed, showing the many awards the winery has received.

This is a good winery to try for a number of reasons, two of which include myth busting. The first myth is that rosés are fruity and sweet. If you run for the German hills (possibly dressed in lederhosen singing with Julie Andrews) at the first sight of anything remotely resembling a White Zinfandel, this might just be the rosé that changes your mind. Gopfrich's rosé, or "Rosa" as he calls it, (meaning red in both German and Latin) is dry and will having you singing "Goodbye, Aufwiedersehen, Goodnight" to any perceptions you might have had about this style of wine.

The second myth that Ray intends to bust is the idea that all Rieslings are sweet. I myself was under this impression since all of the Rieslings I've ever tried were abundantly sweet, almost too over the top. To help bust this myth, Ray goes over in great detail the different between a sweet and dry Riesling, and how you can even tell from the labeling on the bottle. In addition to the tasting, you get a bit of an educational lesson on German wine labels. This is incredibly helpful since German labeling laws require quite a bit of information to be on the bottle for identification. If Ray had not been there to describe in detail what each sentence and phrase meant on the bottle, I'd totally lost. Ray is a great steward for the wine world and I appreciated his in-depth knowledge of wine and wine making.

All of Gopfrich's wines are easily approachable, drinkable wines. You don't have to think too hard to get the smell and taste in the wines. Ray is all smiles when he is pouring his wines. He is proud of his work and is not afraid to boast on occasion. Also, Ray's wines are dependable from year to year. Many of his wine club members take pride in the fact that there is continuity in his work. In addition, very few wines are blended together. Most of the wines are 100% varietal.

The prices of his wines range from the upper teens for the Rosa and the Rieslings, to the lower $40s for the reserve Cabernet Sauvignon (which he keeps in the barrel a year longer).

For a truly international tasting, head over to Gopfrich winery. The one-man-band of Ray Gopfrich is a joy to talk with and will keep you smiling throughout your tasting. Just remember to call in advance and keep in mind that the lederhosen is optional.

Hawley

Location
6387 West Dry Creek Rd.
Healdsburg, CA

Phone
(707) 431-2705

Hours of Operation
Daily approx. 11:00–4:00
By appointment

Tasting Fee
None

In looking at different wine maps, you're often presented with more choices to taste at than restaurants to eat at. And sometimes the real winners are the spaces between the dots. In a land where every three feet sits either a grapevine or an olive tree, chances are good that with grapes come a winery. But not every winery has signs saying, "You're almost there." Some don't have any signs at all. Welcome to Hawley.

Hawley is small, so small that on nearly every wine map I have, the location is not evident. If it weren't for two personal recommendations from other wineries (thank you Nalle and Hafner), I would have kept driving right by the turn-off and would have never found this winery.

When asked how crowded the winery can be, Paul Hawley joked, "This is about as crowded as it usually gets," as he looked at our three-person tasting team. Tastings are conducted by appointment; however, I called the afternoon before and easily found a time the next day. If you do want to taste, I'd suggest being flexible as times could vary depending on who is available to conduct the tasting.

The tasting room at Hawley is in the barrel room. A makeshift table sits about six feet in front of the main door. From there, you can see most of the facility, with the stainless steel tanks, countless barrels and office. Also around are a few different paintings, all done by the wife of the winemaker.

A generous selection of wines were poured for us, including two different Viogniers (vee-ohn-yay). Having rarely seen even a single Viognier being produced in the valley (the wine is out there, but you have to look), I knew that seeing two different ones was a real treat. I can't remember the last time I did a horizontal tasting with Viogniers. The classic lemon taste came out in both, with slight other supportive fruit characteristics in each one.

Along with the Viognier, a Chardonnay rounds out the whites. For the reds, the staple wines of Dry Creek can be found— Zinfandel and Cabernet Sauvignon. Along with those, Hawley also produces a Pinot Noir, a Petite-guaranteed-to-turn-your-teeth-purple Sirah and a Merlot. To finish off the tasting, a late harvest Zinfandel was poured and Paul Hawley (who conducted the tasting) also treated us to a taste of the 2007 Merlot, straight from the barrel.

Hawley is a certified organic vineyard. Along with their desire for sustainability, John and Dana Hawley wanted to keep the grounds fertile, beautiful and healthy for generations to come.

Tasting is complimentary at Hawley. That, coupled with very reasonable prices for the wines (from the lower $20s to upper $30s), make this winery a good value for the quality. The personal stewardship from Paul Hawley in pouring the wine further added to the family quality of this winery.

A fun, off-of-the-main-street, off-of-the-map feeling completely makes Hawley truly shine. Just remember to call first before you make the drive up to ensure you are treated just like family when you are there.

Quivira

Location
4900 West Dry Creek Road
Healdsburg, CA

Phone
(707) 431-8333

Hours of Operation
Daily 11:00–5:00

Tasting Fee
$5
Waived with purchase

Quivira is not hard to miss but it is a little bit off the beaten path. I would venture to say that if you were not traveling on West Dry Creek Road to get to a few other wineries, chances are that you would not even know Quivira was here. Despite being a bit remote, the tasting room sits right off to the side of the road. The roof is lined with solar panels, part of the winery's sustainable culture. The parking lot is small up front and I've found myself parking on the dirt back lot on a few occasions.

The tasting room is very airy, with large glass windows opening to the view of the Quivira grapes in front of you. Small halogen lights mimic the meandering tasting bar and a few assortments dart the back walls behind. The openness of the tasting room becomes apparent the moment you walk in the door.

Quivira prides itself on its sustainable, biodynamic and organic farming practices. On a recent tasting there, I was ecstatic to see the company had begun putting the biodynamic certification logo on the back of its bottles. Biodynamic growing practices are like organic farming taken to the next level—a little bit of science, a few thousand years of growing history and a cow horn go in to make up the biodynamic process. Winemaker Steven Canter says he can even tell if a wine is biodynamic simply by feeling the weight of the bottle. I admit that in a blind tasting, I have been able to tell the difference between a wine grown biodynamically and one grown in the traditional styles, as the wine does feel lighter in a way. But I'm quite far off in being able to tell the difference simply based upon weight.

Along with the biodynamic farming practices, Quivira has also helped restore a nearby creek to help the Steelhead salmon swim upstream and spawn. Quivira's commitment to leaving a lighter footprint on the earth is self-evident in the multitude of sustainable practices it employs.

Back in the tasting room, you're faced with a good selection of wines, including three different Zinfandels. A nominal $5 tasting fee applies, which I feel is fair to taste the wines, and the fee is waived if a bottle is purchased. The pourers are very courteous and answered nearly every answer I threw at them. Many questions I heard around me concerned the biodynamic farming. Smartly, Quivira handily places a small informational sheet with the biodynamic farming information on various spots around the tasting room.

The wines range from the sole white, a sauvignon blanc, to the bold syrah, which they brought back from a year hiatus. During my first tasting there, the pourer even laid out a horizontal tasting of the three Zinfandels, a welcomed sight to a taster. The excitement was because I could then compare the three different Zins side by side. If you are up there on your next tasting, ask the pourer if they will do that for you. It's a great way to see how the three differ and how each one in your party will like something different. Just don't get them confused as you're trying them.

Outside, a slew of benches line the patio with shade coming in two forms, umbrellas and olive trees. During the summer and late spring, when temperatures can hit the triple digits, the shade can be a welcome relief if you are waiting or eating outside. I've personally planned my tasting trips to accommodate lunch underneath the olive trees. And while the winery is close to the road, the small traffic seems to be more white noise than annoying car traffic. While eating lunch outside, chances are good you'll see a handful of bikers go riding by.

Both professional and semi-pro cyclists, along with the novice scenic biker, can be seen on this road, as the small amount of traffic and beautiful views make it a much desired place to ride.

Quivira's prices range from $18 for the Sauvignon Blanc to $34 for their Zinfandel. Head to Quivira for a well-rounded taste of many Dry Creek staple wines and to taste at one of the few biodynamically farmed wineries in the valley.

UNTI

DRY CREEK VALLEY

ZINFANDEL

2 0 0 6

88% ZINFANDEL · 9% PETITE SIRAH · 3% BARBERA

...OWN, PRODUCED AND BOTTLED

...NTI VINEYARDS HEALDSBURG, CA

...HOL 14.5% BY VOLUME

2006 ZIN

VARIETAL
separate block
old Primitivo-c
year old head-pr
clone vineyard b
berries and loose
in old vine Zin. W
vines to help minim

VINTAGE/HARVE
it the best two consec
than a wet spring, 2006
carried into harvest seas
which is no easy task wi
harvest our Zin at physio
making for a full-bodied, y
representative of the Dry C
structure, and balance of ou
much Petite Sirah in 2006 as

VINIFICATION: Grapes we
into both open-top and closed-t
to 5 day cold-soak, are pumped
and pressed immediately upon di
carried out using indigenous yeas
for added texture. Petite Sir
Barbera adds a touch
French oak ha

Unti

Location
4202 Dry Creek Road
Healdsburg, CA

Phone
(707) 433-5590

Hours of Operation
Daily approx. 11:00–4:00
By appointment preferred

Tasting Fee
None

Buried deep in the California wine world is a winery that still draws on its Italian roots. It's hard to believe, but Italy produces more wine than all of the United States. To say that Italians drink wine like water is an understatement.

Lying nearly in the center of Dry Creek is Unti. A simple sign sits out on the road announcing its location. The inside of the tasting room has about the same amount of flair as the sign. A selection of artwork, reminiscent of Italy lines one wall. Different sized prints are available for purchase. On another wall sits a few maps of Italy, which pourers will, at times, point to, to give tasters a location of where the wine making is from. Simple tasting bars on wheels are positioned off to one side and in the back sits the wine barrels.

At times, Mick, or father George Unti, can be seen meandering around the tasting room. A soft-spoken man, George still knows his Italian and if you get him started chatting in Italian, chances are you'll be there for a bit longer than you originally thought. A friend of mine, whom I was tasting with and who had lived in Italy for 15 years, seemed to carry on a conversation for a good part of 10 minutes. She enjoyed the Italian conversation all the while sipping the Italian winemaking style.

At Unti, you're not going to find the wine standards. There is no Chardonnay, Merlot or Cabernet Sauvignon here. Yes, they do make a Zinfandel (did you really think a Dry Creek winery wouldn't?), but they feature wines that you probably have never heard of. Among the list of wines are a Sangiovese and a Grenache. They are probably the only winery in Dry Creek that features a stand-a-lone Mouvedre.

This is a great location to expand your Italian palate and learn a bit more about the various regions of Italy. The pourer will take you on a pseudo-geographical journey around the country of Italy, with the wines being made in the various styles of Italy.

Many of the wines are blends at Unti. And it's easy to figure out what the exact breakdown is in the wine, because they put the percentages right on the front of the label. It's helpful to see it written clearly when the person pouring explains why they used certain grapes for blending.

It never fails to impress me how a simple change in a blend can have such a dramatic effect on the taste of the wine. For example, at the time of this writing, Unti featured two Grenaches. One was a blend with 75% Grenache, 15% Syrah and 10% Mouvedre and the other was blended with the same three grapes, but with more Mouvedre and less Syrah. And while the Syrah and Mouvedre only account for 25% of the blend, the tastes couldn't have been further apart. The pourer referred to these two as GSM and GMS but not MSG.

Appointments are recommended at Unti. You can show up on a whim but if it's crowded, you'll be basically taking a number while the people who called for an appointment get first taste. For reservations, call early. The winery gets busy in the afternoon with its location being directly on Dry Creek Road.

There is no fee to taste at Unti. With a large slew of wines to try, I was impressed at the complimentary price. The wines range from $20 for the rosé to upwards of $50 for the larger bodied wines. The prices for Unti are very reasonable for the caliber of the wines. These wines would be great additions to home cellars for two reasons. They are unique, and mostly all are only available at the winery. While other wineries produce Grenaches and Sangioveses, it is the original blending styles that sets Unti apart.

Unti is a fun departure from the staple varietals of the California wine world. The pourers are very knowledgeable about Unti's winemaking and can answer nearly any question you throw at them. Just don't ask them in Italian, unless you're talking with George.

Family Wineries

Location
4791 Dry Creek Rd.
Healdsburg, CA

Phone
(888) 433-6555

Hours of Operation
Daily 10:30–4:30

Tasting Fee
$5
Waived with purchase

Challenge: Six different vintners all produce distinctly different wines. They're not big enough for each to have its own tasting room but they still want to show off their wines. Solution? Set up Family Wineries, where you can sample from six different wineries, all family-owned and locally grown.

Family Wineries can be found directly off Dry Creek Road, nearly in the center of Dry Creek. It's in the cul-de-sac with two other wineries in this book, Kokomo and Papapietro Perry. If you only have a limited amount of time, I'd recommend stopping here. It's the only multiple-winery tasting room in Dry Creek.

The tasting room is part family store, part hip-tasting counter. All of the wines for taste can be found spread around the room, in between little trinkets and treasures. The pourers here are a gem to chat with. They seem to know more about the valley and other wineries than almost anyone else in the valley (well, ok, maybe not Doug Nalle of Nalle Wine. See page 73)

The first time I was at Family Wineries, I wasn't quite sure what exactly to try. There are more than 20 different varietals to choose from, including a slew of "reserves" on the back of the tasting sheet. One of the people behind the counter could tell I was trying to determine my course of action and asked me what I liked. I was going to say, everything, but that day I had a craving for Syrah. So I explained to her I'm looking for that Rhone style, little pepper, lotta leather deep rooted taste. She chuckled and found three different Syrahs to choose from. She also took the time to explain more about each winery, the style of wine making and other little tidbits.

A little tasting sheet is provided to mark down which ones you want to try or, in my case, make notes about the wines I was trying. While I didn't go this route, I did think about trying most of the wines from one winery and then trying wines from a different winery on another trip. The possibilities are nearly endless.

A beautiful front porch sat unused the time I was there. It's a great location to sit out, look over the central vines in the middle of the valley as well as wave to the Papapietro Perry crowd across the street. I found this winery to have a smaller crowd than some of the traditional tasting rooms in the valley. That said, it always seemed to have at least a handful of people at the tasting bar. This leaves this winery a great spot to hit during peak times of the day, around 2 to 4 p.m.

The wineries featured at Family Wineries are Collier Falls Vineyards, Dashe Cellars, Forth Vineyards, Lago di Merlo Winery and Vineyards, Mietz Cellars and Philip Staley. Each has a different style and taste to its wines. I've tasted everything from bananas in the white wine (yes, I said bananas) to the classic black pepper found in many Dry Creek Zinfandels.

In addition to the standards of Chardonnay, Merlot, Cabernet Sauvignon and Zinfandel, Family Wineries has some varietals you might have never tried or even heard of before. Some of the lesser known wines include Grenache, Primitivo, Semillon and a Petit Verdot. Of course, with six different wineries, you're bound to find and taste some wonderful surprises.

The prices are very reasonable, with some of the wines dropping into the teens. Overall, I'd say the bulk run in the upper $20s to mid $30s. Of course, prices can fluctuate so use these prices as a guide. The cost for wine tasting is $5 and is refundable with purchase of any wine.

Kokomo

Location
4791 Dry Creek Road
Healdsburg, CA

Phone
(707) 433-0200

Hours of Operation
Daily 11:00–4:30

Tasting Fee
$5
Waived with purchase

The wine industry is full of iconography—leaves, grapes, de-stemmers and an occasional Riedel® glass for good measure. They all make up the vast bottle designs and logos (okay, so maybe not the de-stemmer) in the wine world. Adding to the vast list of icons is now a cypress tree, the logo for Kokomo Winery. The name of the winery has its roots (truly no pun intended there) in Kokomo, Indiana where winemaker Erik Miller began his trek to the Russian river.

Tasting at Kokomo, you immediately notice the tall stacks of barrels behind the person pouring. That's because the tasting room triples as a storage facility as well as the production room where the wine is made. Light accessories dart the walls around the tasting area. While it is not that uncommon for tasting rooms to feature the barrel storage area (after all, might as well cool two birds with one stone), the upfront pseudo wall of the barrels is truly the first thing you'll notice when you walk in.

The wines range from two whites, a Sauvignon Blanc and a Chardonnay, and a slew of red wines made from grapes grown in many different regions, including Chalk Hill, Russian River Valley and the Sonoma coast. It was a pleasure to try the same type of wine from different regions to get a sense of just how different climates, soils and elevations can affect the taste. Also, Kokomo is one of the few wineries that is producing a 100% Cabernet Sauvignon. I recommend that if you are a Cabernet Sauvignon fan you try this wine. It's a hidden rarity in Dry Creek. Also, if you are a fan of your Syrahs tasting like white pepper was literally ground into the wine, you will also be in for a treat.

What surprised me the most was that the color did not dictate the intensity in any way. I was shocked when the lighter wines, literally nearing rosé shades, packed more of a punch than a Mike Tyson right-hand. The deep, can't see you're fingers underneath the glass, red blend, was subtle in taste, much like the intensity of a ballet dancer. The pourer sensed I was quickly sizing up the soon-to-be-tasted wine by looking at the color and warned me of the impending strength.

The entire fleet of wines is a good representation of what Dry Creek and the greater Sonoma county is producing. From the slightly oaked Chardonnay all the way down to the big Petite Sirah and Zinfandel.

The tasting fee is $5 and you can pick five wines to try from the list. The prices range from $16 for the Sauvignon Blanc to $36 for the Malbec. With most of the wines coming in the lower $20s, nearly all of their wines hit a sweet spot on price.

Kokomo is in the tasting cul-de-sac that features a few other wineries and is directly off Dry Creek Road. It's easy to pick out the tasting room by the large red building and black sign featuring the beloved cypress tree. If you are looking for a new winery on the block to try, I'd recommend Kokomo. The staff is friendly, the wines are easy to enjoy and they deliver some wonderful hallmarks of the Dry Creek staple grapes.

Papapietro Perry

Location
4791 Dry Creek Road
Healdsburg, CA

Phone
(877) GO PINOT

Hours of Operation
Daily 11:00–4:30

Tasting Fee
$5

When wine tasting in the Dry Creek Valley, the Pinot Noir is usually found more in the dictionary than on most tasting room counters. Only 162 acres of grapes in the valley are Pinot. While that may sound pretty large, the most widely planted grape, Cabernet Sauvignon, stands at 2,316 acres. With the valley's hot days and dryer conditions, the finicky pinot grape yearns for cooler temps and moderately warm afternoons. So it was a bit of a surprise to hear of a winery in the Dry Creek area bottling a Pinot Noir.

Papapietro Perry sits on a small hill with a few other tasting rooms sharing the cul-de-sac. It's in a good location to try other wineries within walking distance (well, it all depends on how far you're willing to walk). Walking in to Papapietro Perry's winery, you immediately run directly into the bar. The smaller room means that on a busy day, you could be hanging out by the door. But don't let that deter you from some serious wines.

I say serious because the phrases on Papapietro's clothing is anything but. I'm constantly amazed at the wine/sexual innuendo combinations that wineries come up with. While I have seen a shirt here or there with a catchy and witty phrase, I'd say that Papapietro Perry takes the cake on this one. A bit indicative of the wine, one shirt reads, "Long lasting, with a big finish." Another shirt, "So good you'll want to swallow". I enjoy wineries that throw a bit of humor around. It seems to soften the oftentimes lofty feel of a tasting room.

The tasting bar nearly spans the entire width of the room. The bronze countertop matches, according to a Dunn Edwards paint swatch book, a dirty apricot color. Behind the bar were a few bottles, lightly decorated with plants and other accessories.

While they have produced a Chardonnay in the past, Papapietro Perry is all about two varietals—Pinot Noir and Zinfandel. The strength of the wines comes from the location. Papapietro Perry seeks out some of Sonoma County's prime growing areas for the grapes. And when you are poured a Pinot Noir, you are getting 100% Pinot Noir. No 85% or 90%. Just pure Pinot.

The strength of winemaking comes out in the wines. The Pinot Noirs had both Old World, deep terroir and smoke in the taste, and new world characteristics such as being more fruit driven. If you want to experience different smells and tastes coming from the same grape (though grown in different locations), this would be the place to stop at to get your Pinot fill.

I can best describe the Zinfandel as being one of those new freight locomotives. They are quiet but pack a serious punch under the hood. The pepper aspect is clearly present on the wines and with a long finish (just like the t-shirt promotes); it can be tasted for nearly a minute after swallowing. With the two Zins coming out of two different areas, this is a great place to see how the region can affect the taste of the same grape.

And for serious wine, you need serious stemware. At Papapietro Perry, all of their wines are poured in Riedel® glasses designed for the varietals you're tasting. If you are new to the craziness of stemware, I should let you know that Riedel© makes nearly a different glass for each type of wine, from Chardonnay to Pinot Noir. It's a great complement to the winery and a great addition to tasting this wine. While this isn't such a big issue elsewhere, I have been to wineries where the glass is so small at the top that I've strained my nose squeezing into that small opening just to get a whiff of the wine.

With bigger wines come moderately bigger prices. The wines range from the lower $30s to around $70 for one of the Pinots. With many of their wines receiving more than 90+ points in various wine magazines, the prices are reflective of the quality. For some of the strongest Pinots around, head over to Papapietro Perry. Warning: Drinking the wine might cause pinot envy elsewhere.

Nalle

Location
2383 Dry Creek Rd.
Healdsburg, CA

Phone
(707) 433-1040

Hours of Operation
Sat. 12:00–5:00

Tasting Fee
$5
Waived with purchase

Laughter, knowledge, good and great wine. Four words to describe Nalle Winery.

When driving up to Nalle, be sure to look for the sign, since it's about two feet long and what seems to be six inches high. A tasting sign with hours can usually be spotted immediately below it. What the sign lacks in physical size, the winery's building makes up for in uniqueness. The tasting room/wine storage area/impromptu basketball game area is trapezoidal-shaped, with rosemary growing off the top three sides. It's hard to miss when traveling south on Dry Creek Road. The shape of the interior is actually cylindrical, a half circle in all. The Nalles call this their "potato bunker." They describe the building as "a peaceful place to age wine with zero heating or cooling units." I was surprised to feel the appropriate "wine chill" when I walked in, even as it was quite warm outside. You might also see the Nalles' dog, Henry, meandering in and out of the "potato bunker."

For over a quarter of a century, Doug Nalle has been making Zinfandel in Dry Creek. In a land where Zinfandel is king, Doug is one of the forerunners.

His knowledge and experience comes out in conversations. I've oftentimes wondered why I didn't bring a digital recorder to log some of Doug's engaging dialogs. With each tasting, you'll get more than information on the nose and tannins, you'll receive a mini-history on the way the wine was made, right from the winemaker. Every time I'm there, I seem to learn something new.

Questions are welcomed and appreciated here. And if you have any questions about wine, this would be the place to ask them. Wine tasting can and should be as much of an educational experience as it is an entertaining one.

Along with education comes a bit of humor. While Nalle does take wine seriously, they do have a humorous side. From the yearly cartoons that feature play-on-words to Zinfandel (such as Siamese Zins) to the labeling of one of their recent bottles, "Good Wine," you're sure to smile from the simple humor found in Nalle.

There is a $5 tasting fee, a standard for the Dry Creek region. The fee is waived with the purchase of any bottle of wine. The wines are in the $30 to $40 range. I found the real deal to be the limited reserves that can be found on a side table. Some wineries charge in the triple digits for ten year plus wines, especially Cabernet Sauvignons. Nalle's prices are only slightly more expensive than the current releases, about $20 to $30 more, depending on how old the wine is. And Nalle's wines can go the distance. Lay it down or drink it the afternoon after purchasing, the wines are great.

Aside from the Dry Creek standard of Zinfandel, Nalle also produces a Pinot Noir as well as a Chardonnay. Due to the smaller size of this winery, do not be surprised if they are sold out of certain wines. Never fear though, because chances are good the next vintage will be as good as the last.

A unique and often overlooked aspect of Nalle's wines is that the alcohol content is much lower than typical California standards. In today's world, it's common to easily see 16% and up in alcohol. As I was tasting, Doug pointed out that the reason for the 750ml bottle size is so two people can have two glasses of wine without feeling tipsy topsy. I appreciate that as I do consume quite a bit of wine.

Another wonderful courtesy at Nalle is that they are very open to you bringing wine you've previously purchased in to their tasting room to store it inside while tasting. With Dry Creek easily reaching triple digits on spring and summer days, this is a welcome relief to the wine.

Look for Nalle's "potato bunker" just off of Dry Creek Rd. It's not difficult to miss if you are coming south, as it stands out very clearly. For some well-made wine and a bit of humor, head over to Nalle.

Pezzi King

Location
3225 West Dry Creek Road (Winery)
Healdsburg, CA

Phone
(707) 431-9388

Hours of Operation
Weekends approx. 11:00–4:00
By appointment

Tasting Fee
None

If there were an oasis in this desert we call Dry Creek, Pezzi King would be it. The drive is barren, half-paved with the other half on dirt and rocks. There is no large flashy sign designating how many gold medals or hours of operation. In fact, the only indicator of the turnoff to Pezzi King is the mailbox number. However, much like an oasis, the interior is much more lush and barren turns to beautiful.

There are two locations to taste Pezzi King's wine. At the time of this writing, the winery was working on a downtown Healdsburg tasting room, soon to be completed (in fact, by the time you are reading this, chances are good that it is open). The other location, nestled high in the Dry Creek hillside, is the personal residence of Mr. James P Rowe Sr. and accompanying vineyards where the heart of Pezzi King is.

At the personal residence, wine tastings are conducted pool-side at either the cabana-resembling bar or the lounge chairs and sofas lying around one side of the pool. Reily, the owners' dog, can often be found lounging by the feet of the tasting party.

The grounds are immaculately-groomed and the vistas are unparalleled, with rows and rows of grapes extending as far as the eye can see, all the way across the valley floor. A fountain provided a beautiful background noise in conjunction with the outdoor stereo. The songs of Frank Sinatra sung by Harry Connick Jr. further made it a relaxed atmosphere. It was such a comfortable setting that I even called my next appointment and pushed it back an extra hour, knowing I was not going to rush through this tasting. In addition to drinking the wine, a food and cheese plate was presented to me and my tasting partner. It was a beautiful and rarely seen addition to a wine tasting. The other unexpected treat of the day was that the owner, Jim, came down and chatted with us about his winery.

Tasting at the personal residence is only by appointment, so do remember to call ahead if you want to come up there. Also, give yourself a few extra minutes to drive up the one-way street off West Dry Creek Road. It is easy to veer off in the wrong direction if you are not paying attention since the winery is only marked by address numbers, not the name of the company.

Pezzi King's wines are equally beautiful. Utilizing all 70 acres, the wines run the gamut, from Sauvignon Blanc and Chardonnay to Merlot, Cabernet Sauvignon, Pinot Noir and Zinfandel. All of Pezzi King's wines showed a wonderful mouth feel and were overall smooth tasting. Nearly all of these wines could be opened the next day, with the one exception being the Cabernet Sauvignon. A surprise was the fruit-forward Sauvignon Blanc. Generally, the Sauvignon Blancs of the region are more acidic, evoking a lemon-grass taste in your mouth rather than mangos and pineapples.

Another treat was tasting both a Zinfandel and an old vine Zin. If you have never tried an old vine Zin, you will be in for a treat. While the newer vine Zinfandel is a joy to drink in its own way, the old-vine Zinfandel is more of a straight punch to your taste buds. The older, and wiser, vines show their wisdom by displaying soft tannins while still displaying the spiciness that one comes to expect from a Zinfandel.

At the time of this writing, there was no charge for tasting at the personal residence. The prices for the wines are average for the region, with the Sauvignon Blanc priced at $18, the mid-range wines around $30 and the reserves and limited productions at $50 and up.

Time truly will slow down while you are tasting at Pezzi King. The comfortable chairs, ambient music and the über-relaxed Reily will aide in your tranquility on top of the wine tasting. Pezzi King is an oasis in this Dry Creek Valley.

Montemaggiore

ROSÉ

DRY CREEK VALLEY · SONOMA COUNTY

PAOLO'S VINEYARD · SYRAH 100%

ESTATE GROWN 2007

Montemaggiore

Location
2355 West Dry Creek Rd.
Healdsburg, CA

Phone
(707) 433-9499

Hours of Operation
Daily approx. 11:00–4:00
By appointment

Tasting Fee
None

In the Dry Creek region, one type of wine reigns supreme—Zinfandel. Second only to Cabernet Sauvignon, this wine can be found at nearly every winery in the area, with the exception of one—Montemaggiore (pronounced mohn tay ma JOHR ray). It is here where you find that the king of the land, Zinfandel, takes a back seat to another, lessor grown grape in the valley—Syrah.

Montemaggiore sits on the southwest corner of the Dry Creek Region. The winery is truly a mom and pop operation, with Vince Ciolino growing the grapes and wife Lise producing the wine.

Montemaggiore is open only by appointment so plan accordingly if you want to taste here. Also, there is no sign on the road, just a mailbox number indicating where to turn. When I called, Vince helped out greatly by providing me with literally turn-by-turn directions once I veered off West Dry Creek Road. So while it might be a tad more difficult to find than wineries on the main street, it is nonetheless manageable to get up there.

The tasting room is literally situated in the bottling/de-stemming/barrel room. A simple round glass bar is used for the tasting. A little book is provided for you with room to write notes and information about the wines. With so many Syrahs, it comes in handy.

Montemaggiore's wines are all made organically and biodynamically. Biodynamic farming takes organic farming to an extreme. Visually, you can see the biodynamic farming take place with the sheep grazing the hillside and the female cow's horn sitting to the side of the tasting bar. The biodynamic farming practices are a mixture of science, phases of the moon and a little bit of voodoo.

As mentioned above, Montemaggiore is all about Syrah. If there was ever a place to sing the lines from Doris Day's "Que Sera, Sera," this would be it. The entire tasting was comprised around this beloved grape. For Syrah newbies, this is a great place to experience both 100% Syrah as well as Syrah/Cabernet Sauvignon blends. Each year Vince and Lise produce a Syrah with a different Syrah/Cab combo.

For example, their '04 Superiore is 70% Cabernet and 30% Syrah (remember, you can't call the wine a Cab or a Syrah since neither grape breaches the 75% mark), while their '04 Paolo's Vineyard Syrah (named after their son) is comprised of 95% Syrah and 5% Cab.

When I was there last, Vince set up a vertical tasting, allowing me and my tasting partner to fully experience a different Syrah from year to year. All three wines, the '03, '04 and '05, had different characteristics.

There was no charge to taste the wines and all the them were between $25 and $45, which is comparable to other wineries' prices. A rosé can also be found, made from, you guessed it, Syrah grapes. It's one of the only rosés I've seen that come from that grape. Also, half bottles are available for purchase on select wines.

If your palate has had more Zinfandels than you care to admit, a detour over to Montemaggiore can be a pleasant change. I'm sure that you too will soon be singing the new lines, "Que Syrah, Syrah," upon sampling this luscious selection of the very grape.

Alexander Valley

Sonoma County's "hidden valley". Alexander Valley is one of the easiest regions to get to. On the west side of the valley is Highway 101. To the East sits Calistoga and the Northern end of Napa Valley. Yet looking at the foot traffic Clistoga gets in comparison to its neighboring wine region, Alexander Valley, its like night and day.

The wine of Alexander Valley is similar to that of Northern Napa Valley and the Russian River. Lush Chardonnays with hints of oak and butter. Deep Cabernet Sauvignon's that seem to contain bit of cocoa and tobacco. In addition to the wines mentioned above, you'll find Merlots, a few Zins and if you look carefully, a few Bordeaux blends.

The climate is a bit cooler out here, with fog in the morning and slowly burning off during the day to allow for the sun to shine over countless rows of grapes. The wineries in this region are spread out and tucked away into the rolling hills.

Time seems to slow down a bit when you enter into this valley. The staff at many of the wineries see you more as a welcomed patron than someone who just wants to drink, buy and leave. Out here, smiles seem to last longer and the enjoyment of wine tasting seems just a bit richer.

Welcome to Alexander Valley.

Route 128

Location
21079 Geyserville Ave.
Geyserville, CA

Phone
(707) 696-0004

Hours of Operation
Thurs. – Mon. 11:00–6:00

Tasting Fee
None

A new winery has moved into the town of Geyserville. Its name is Route 128 Winery. Like a newly polished car, this winery shines, from the "Now Open" sign glistening in the sun outside to the well placed artwork along two of the walls in the "tasting parlor." While the winery may be new, the experience behind the company is extensive.

Route 128 Winery's tasting parlor is cozy and very friendly. The tasting room sits on—where else—Route 128 in downtown Geyserville. The downtown region of Geyserville is about three blocks long, so it's not hard to find this winery. It sits on the northern end of the few blocks, close to Meeker and Locals.

Inside, a few barstools are available to eager tasters along with a couple other chairs toward the back of the room. Modern artwork by a local artist is showcased, which gives the parlor a sense of warmth and good energy. Behind the tasting counter are a few different bottles of wine along with a back-lit sign of the company's name. Other little items for sale can be found dotting the room. For how small the room is, the owners did a great job of maximizing the space.

The husband and wife owned winery is based out of Cloverdale, about a 10-15 minute drive north from downtown Geyserville. Their grapes come from both the estate (pictures of their grapevines can be seen in the tasting parlor) along with vineyards in the Russian River and Alexander Valley. Lorna, the wife of the winemaker, was pouring for me the day I was in. I could tell she was very proud of the wine they produce and was very open on how well the wine was tasting. Her candid remarks over the uncertainty of one of the wines made the tasting that much more intimate. I've rarely heard someone, especially the owner, speak with such forthright.

Route 128 produces quite a selection of wines, including a Viognier, a Zinfandel, a Pinot Noir, a Cabernet Sauvignon and a Syrah. All of them faired remarkably well, considering how young the winery is. The two wines that stood out for me were the Viognier and the Syrah.

The Viognier was one of the strongest ones I've tasted in a while. I tasted a bit of pear and peach in this fruit driven wine. The length (the taste of the wine after you've swallowed or spit it out) kept going on for a while, maybe about a minute or so. It's a trait that isn't seen too much in Viogniers, for they usually pack a good punch but fade quickly afterwards. This was a very well made wine.

The Syrah was equally bold, but on a whole other level. It featured hints of dark chocolate and blueberries. Lorna informed me that when it was first bottled (I tasted the '04), the wine had the freshest aromas of blueberries she'd ever smelled, as if someone had baked a blueberry pie. A little spiciness topped it off to make it a well-rounded wine. I'm quite curious to see how this one will age, as it has already gone through quite a transformation.

The prices for the wines range from $26 for the Viognier to $30 for the Cab and Pinot Noir. There is no charge for tasting. The tasting parlor is closed on Tuesday and Wednesday, so any mid-week tasters are out of luck. Most of the smaller wineries will either close their doors during the week or at least be closed on Mondays, so this shift in schedule can be a great advantage if you are tasting outside of the weekend.

If you ever plan to motor west, looking for a wine country that is the best, I'm sure you'll get your kicks, at Route…128 Winery.

Meeker

Location
21035 Geyserville Avenue
Geyserville, CA

Phone
(707) 431-2148

Hours of Operation
Mon. - Sat. 10:30-6:00
Sunday 12:00-5:00

Tasting Fee
None

One of the joys of wine tasting, aside from drinking the wine, is the ambiance. I've seen wineries that feature travertine marble, impeccably manicured lawns and the most magnificent gates greeting you upon arrival. I've often wondered if the symphony, dressed in full tuxedos, is awaiting me upon opening the door. And while that is wonderful, I often like the smaller wineries, the ones with squeaky doors where you are treated more like family and after a few trips you're greeted by name. And then there is Meeker.

Meeker's tasting room sits inside a historic bank. They've kept as much of the inside of the building intact as possible. Behind and to the side of the tasting bar are the old teller windows. Where the business end of the bank was once conducted now sits the business end of the winery. Because it is literally set up the same way, visitors to Meeker walk along the same lines as waiting depositors back in the day did. As with any bank building, there's a safe. But this one holds no money.

The safe here is filled with wine. What better place to store your wine than in a room encased with nearly a foot thick of steel on all sides? When the person pouring the wines told me about that, I didn't believe him. In walking over to the safe, I found out he was telling the truth. Along with keeping an even temperature, I figured it is pretty secure against theft.

Meeker's website boasts that this is the "most creative tasting room in Sonoma County." And while the jury is still out for me, I will say that they are in the top ten. Meeker used to conduct tastings inside of an authentic Sioux tipi back in the 1980s. Yet due to demand and Sonoma County's threat to close down the tipi for lack of a tasting room permit, the Meeker vineyard's tasting room has moved around and currently settled in the town of Geyserville. A picture of the tasting room tipi can been seen on one of the walls in the current tasting room and plans are being conceived to bring back the tipi. I, for one, can't wait.

If the thought of possibly tasting wine in a vault doesn't make you chuckle, the design of the labels on the bottles will. While there is serious wine making here, the look of the bottles might lead you to believe otherwise. As an artist, I loved the myriad of designs presented on the various bottles. From a beach theme on the Chardonnay to a picture of a longhorn and a flag of Texas on the Cabernet Sauvignon, the designs reach out in all different directions. My favorite design was for the 2005 Dry Creek Valley Winemaker's Reserve Zinfandel. It's probably the most modern design I've seen on a wine label with the bold colors and the hip-hop inspired typography (did I mention I'm a graphic designer?).

Overall, the wines held up very well. Some had a bit more tannins than I would have cared for, however I imagine that given enough time laying down in the cellar, the tannins would soften and become smooth. The tasting list was fairly extensive. It ranged from a dry rosé, to a late harvest dessert wine, appropriately named, "Fro Zin."

I'd have to say that the wines were a bit off of the beaten path, much like the history and style of Meeker. The wines were good, just not what I was expecting to taste in more common wines, such as with the rosé. This a positive and can be a welcome surprise if you've been dumping black pepper on your tongue all day from tasting Zins in Dry Creek. The prices of the wines range from the lower $20s to the $50s for the bigger reds.

Locals

Location
21023A Geyserville Avenue
Geyserville, CA

Phone
(707) 857-4900

Hours of Operation
Daily 11:00–6:00

Tasting Fee
None

Problem: You're traveling with a group of friends and everyone has a different preference when it comes to wine tasting. One person will only drink whites, another scoffs at anything other than the Bordeaux blends and you like lighter reds, such as a Sangiovese. Solution: Locals. It's a tasting room that pours wines from 10 different wineries. The wines are broken down into varietals, thus satisfying all of your party in one stop (even the Bordeaux addict).

The tasting room's style and upscale decor felt more aligned with the feel of downtown Healdsburg than Geyserville. Nevertheless, it is still beautiful inside, with all of the different wineries' bottles scattered around along with various olive oils, t-shirts and maps. A bright orange sign outside welcomes you in, with interior walls to match.

Once you've stepped up to the bar, you're given a double-sided tasting sheet. With over 62 individual wines to choose from, its a bit overwhelming at first. But the saving grace comes, as I mentioned above, in the fact that tastes are broken up into varietal flights. Meaning that you choose the style of wine that you'd like to try, say Chardonnays, and they'll pour all of the wine together in a row, allowing you to sample them together. Locals also puts the wine bottle behind the glass so you'll always know what winery you're drinking from.

This comes in handy if you've picked the varietal with a bunch of wines in it, such as the Zinfandel with seven different wines or the "Other Reds" that tops out at eight. It's also fun to see how the different bottle designs look compared with one another. And above all, it's fun to compare how the same type of wine can still taste so different, all coming from nearly the same region. The person pouring the wine will probably instruct you to not finish the glass and instead move around from glass to glass letting your palate get a cacophony of flavors.

Some of the flights feature just one wine from each vineyard. Other times, you might get two different wines (same varietal still) from the same vineyard enabling you to see how the same winery, growing grapes in two or three different regions, can produce wines of different tastes.

Being more picky when it comes to Syrah, I decided to try that flight. With only three to choose from, I bounced around comparing two at a time until I came to the conclusion that I liked two out of the three. One of them just didn't hit my taste buds correctly. And no, I'm not revealing which of the three was less preferable. Chances are good you might come to a different conclusion and like the exact opposite of what I would have picked. And that is the main reason why I recommend this place. Subtle differences in the wine will turn on some people and turn off others. But with so many wines to choose from, I'm sure you're bound to satisfy everyone in your party one way or another.

The tasting room is open every day of the week and there is no charge to taste the wines. That's a wonderful value that should not be overlooked here, especially with the number of wines available to taste. The prices run the gamut, from the teens to over $50. Also, be aware that because Locals is pouring wine from smaller vineyards, the exact wines being poured will change more frequently. So if you find a bottle that you like, waiting until the next time you come up to buy might not be the best idea.

Also, this would be a great place to sign up for a wine club membership. The reason why I'd recommend the membership here is variety. While a single vineyard wine club only ships their wine, Locals will bundle different wineries' together, enabling you to try different wines from different wineries. It can be a true treat to be surprised in what they put in each shipment. For complete information on wine club information, talk with one of the staff members at Locals. They can go over the pricing and information with you. (For information on wine clubs in general, see the appendix.)

For a different twist on the single vineyard tasting, check out Locals. I'm sure you'll find some wine you're bound to fall in love with along with satisfying your entire tasting party, including that Bordeaux addict.

Hafner

Location
Call for location

Phone
(707) 433-4606

Hours of Operation
1st & 3rd Friday at 2:00
By appointment

Tasting Fee
None

A barn sits on the far east side of the Alexander Valley. Tucked into the hills and with no sign aside from an address number, it sits humbly away from the hustle and bustle of the main thoroughfare that is route 128. There isn't even a map on this winery's web site indicating how to find it. But while the location might be part of the mystery, the family aspect is clear from the very moment you pick up the phone to call Hafner Vineyards.

Hafner Vineyards is located just off route 128 on the east side of Alexander Valley. While I do have a dot on the map for the location, I've purposely left off the exact location. That is because the Hafners give it to you upon confirming your appointment. I will say that it is about 10-15 minutes off Highway 101 and about 20 minutes outside downtown Healdsburg.

The property is just that, a winery. A long wine cave has been built into the hillside, allowing for all of the wine to age perfectly still. All of the bottles were nearly perfectly aligned in the cave. I was amazed at the attention to detail. Outside of the cave is an old barn that has been converted into office space on the second floor and the ground floor handles the wine making and distribution. An illustration of the barn can be found on the labels, web site and other promotional material. There is no "tasting room" per se, as Hafner only does wine tasting by appointment.

And those appointments only come by twice a month, so plan your trip early if you want to visit Hafner Vineyards. The two tastings are on the first and third Fridays of the month at 2 pm. The winery tries to keep the numbers on the appointments fairly low to give it a more personable feel. The tasting appointments are part tour of the facility and part tasting. Due to the small numbers in the tasting party, the tasting party was intimate. It was easy to get to know Sarah Hafner (the wife of winemaker Parke) as she answered all our questions.

Sarah took us around the property explaining in a wonderfully educational way, the style of winemaking that Hafner incorporates. She explained everything, from the explanation of malolactic fermentation to the type of oak in the barrels they barrel the wine in. I especially enjoyed barrel tasting in the wine cave. This was the first time I've ever done both together, so I was ecstatic. Sarah also poured one of their bottled wines to show the difference between a young, barely in the barrel wine and the wine once it has already been bottled.

Hafner vineyards is a family owned and operated winery, with Parke as the winemaker, Sarah as the graphic designer and Scott Hafner in charge of marketing. Chances are good that you'll hear Scott's voice on the other line when you call to make an appointment.

Hafner Vineyards produces two different wines, a Chardonnay and a Cabernet Sauvignon. They also grow Petit Verdot (pronounced pee-teet verr-dooh) which is used as a blending agent for the Cab. The Chardonnays (they make two) are hallmark Californian. Rich butter cream could be felt in the mouth along with that classic oak—as Gary Vaynerchuk of Wine Library TV calls it, "The Oak Monster." There is not an overbearing of oak, just enough to tickle the taste buds. Given how much butter (yes, think buttered popcorn here) the wine had, I found it fairly dry.

The Cabernets are simply gorgeous right out of the bottle. Little tannins could be felt in the mouth, but far less than I expected for a four-year barrel-aged wine. They were deep in color and complexity (but isn't that the whole point of a Cabernet Sauvignon anyway?) with some leather and dark chocolate, especially at the end after you've swished it around your mouth for a few seconds. Both the Chardonnay and the Cab produce a wondrous mouth feel.

Overall, the wines are refined and beautiful. For someone who loves a good California-style Chardonnay or a deep Cab, this is the place to go. Prices range from $32 for the Chardonnay to a few hundred dollars for a set or vertical flight of wine. The Cabernet Sauvignon goes through four years of cellaring (most wineries cellar, or age the wine, for 18-24 months) before bottled and sold.

Hafner Vineyards is a wonderful winery to taste exquisite wine and learn a bit about the winemaking process at the same time. Just remember to plan early and be aware of the two tasting times. I'm sure you'll leave smiling and satisfied after visiting and wine tasting at Hafner Vineyards.

Johnson's Alexander Valley Wines

Location
8333 Highway 128
Healdsburg, CA

Phone
(707) 433-2319

Hours of Operation
Daily 11:00–5:00

Tasting Fee
None

Johnson's winery is located on the main strip of Alexander Valley, between White Oak (no, not Silver Oak) and Hanna. A weather-worn sign sits out front, a forerunner to the rest of the property. A long road half-paven leads you to the farm house tasting room that is Johnson's Alexander Valley Winery.

The grounds feel like it is someone's personal residence. An old tractor can be seen resting off to the side of the building, while garden gnomes are sprinkled around the property. I felt like I was on a country farm than in the heart of Alexander Valley.

The inside of the tasting room felt much like the outside— rustic. An old wood burning iron stove, a worn-out barber's pole (about 2 feet tall) and all of the wood felt like it had been there for at least half of a century if not longer.

The real treat though, aside from the wine, is the 1924 pipe organ, which is in full working condition. Two sides of the tasting room are filled with a combination of the organ and various accompanying instruments, which included a xylophone and cymbals.

When I first walked in, I felt that the organ had not been run since the '30s. However, I was shocked to actually hear the massive machine suddenly take to life, breathing in volumes of air as if it was preparing to sing at the top of its lungs.

And sing it did. Yet not to the tune of a period piece set back in the roaring twenties. But, I guess, judging by my age and tasting partner, the operator selected a more appropriate tune—the soundtrack of Star Wars. Yes. Star Wars. This has to be the first time I've tasted wine, in a tasting room, all the while visions of Darth Vader, Tatooine and George Lucas were going through my head.

Back at the tasting bar, you're given two wines to try, complimentary— a Chardonnay and a Riesling. They also make a Cabernet Sauvignon, according to the tasting sheet, yet it was sold out. The Chardonnay rolled in at $18, and the Riesling commanded a bargain price of $8.

As I mentioned prior, I felt like I had stepped out of the wine country and onto a country farm. The person pouring made me feel like family. The rustic appeal seemed to have slowed time down and the organ further added to the relaxed atmosphere. Although it was Star Wars playing on the organ, I did stop to listen and took a bit more time to enjoy the tasting experience. For a slight departure from the norm, head over to Johnson's Alexander Valley Winery.

Vérité / Archipel

Location
4611 Thomas Road
Healdsburg, CA

Phone
(800) 273-0177

Hours of Operation
Mon. - Sat. 10:00–5:00
By appointment

Tasting Fee
$25
Waived with purchase

I believe one of the hallmarks of a great chef is his knowledge of how ingredients work together. With the right usage of different spices and condiments, what would be considered a boring dish suddenly springs to life through the hands of the cooking maestro. And just like a great chef, a winemaker's knowledge in how to blend grapes separates the good from the great. Enter stage left—Vérité.

Vérité sits on one of the most southern points of the Alexander Valley. It's so far south that even the "Welcome to Alexander Valley" sign is north of it and on a completely different road altogether. If you are thinking about going to Vérité, the best advice I can give you is to plan ahead, get a map, and give yourself some drive time. With its proximity at least 15 minutes from any major highway and the twisty road leading up to its location, you're bound to be doing a little bit of driving. Also, if you are thinking of doing some wine hopping starting with Vérité, I have some bad news for you. Unlike other wineries that are within a grapes throw of each other, Vérité sits nearly alone on Chalk Hill Road. Only a few other wineries dot this remote street, and they, too, are all appointment only. But do not let the distance be a barrier to some of the strongest Bordeaux blends this side of Napa.

The tasting room of Vérité's is very contemporary, with large high-back chairs around two large tables. Various images of the vineyards along with gorgeous product shots and wooden boxes bearing the wineries' name can be seen around the room. I found it intriguing that the room's decor had such a modern flair since the wine is completely the opposite. At Vérité, the wine bar is more of a distant image as the tasting is conducted at one of the large tables in the room. It's one of the few wineries that features a sit-down tasting in the valley. That's a good thing, for the wines can make you weak in the knees.

Remember I mentioned earlier to plan ahead? That is not only for your schedule, but for Vérité's as well. Vérité opens and lets the wines sit overnight to let the oxygen bring the wines to life. I try to call a day before the day of my reservation, confirming that I am coming and the size of my party. It would be troublesome to have Vérité plan on a group of four only to discover a few minutes prior that the size has grown to eight.

The tasting starts with a brief education about the vines and soil samples. It's a great Cliff Notes education about stressed vines, rocky soil and checking the sugar content in the grapes. I seem to take out a little more each time I'm there for a tasting. Part of the tasting time takes place right outside at one of the rows of grapevines.

Following the lesson in growing the grapes, you're seated around one of the large tables, depending on how large the tasting party is. In front of you are six pre-poured glasses of wine: one glass of the Archipel, three glasses of a recently released trio of Vérité wines and two 1998 released wines from Vérité. Below each glass is a circle denoting the glass placement and the wine you are drinking with the corresponding year.

Off to the side are tasting notes. These are not the general information about how lush and beautiful the wine tastes, but rather the breakdown of the blend of each wine, the points that Robert Parker Jr. gave it (Robert seems to really like Vérité, giving them all 92+ each year) and a little background of how the wine was made. The tastes and smells of each wine are purposefully left off of the notes so that you may decide for yourself what you smell and taste. It's refreshing to not read about what I'm going to taste and smell because it really pushes your palate to find what you pick up. Also, a pen or pencil is provided so that you may make your own notes about each of the wines.

Vérité produces one style of wine—a Bordeaux blend. The name comes from the region of France. Just as most wineries don't use the term Champagne on their bottles, such is the case of a Bordeaux blend. Some wineries will list the various grape combinations on their bottle to denote the kind of wine. Others will just create a new name, such as the case with Vérité. Their three wines are, La Joie, The Muse and Desir. The Archipel is a separate label altogether, but still a Bordeaux blend. All the wines, while made to hit that Bordeaux taste, are different blends of grapes. Generally, Bordeaux blends are composed of three different grapes, Cabernet Sauvignon, Merlot and Cabernet Franc. However, other grapes are used to vary the taste, much like a master chef uses different spices to bring out the taste in a dish.

The wine educator, as the business card title implies, instructs you to taste in a particular order. Generally starting with the Archipel and then moving around the board. This is also a great opportunity to do both a horizontal and a vertical tasting.

A horizontal tasting is where you taste the same vintage of wine but of different blends. Such is the case with Vérité because you are offered up three different Bordeaux blends. A good idea to do here is to taste the wine and then reference the different combinations of grapes. It is really interesting to see how three wines from the same year can taste so different coming from the same winemaker.

A vertical tasting is where you taste the same wine from different years. At my latest tasting, I was offered the three wines from the '02 vintage and then the default two wines from 1998. Vérité provides the vertical tasting so you can see how the wine will evolve and mature over time. While the tasting may be an '03 or another year close to that time period, they always provide you with their older vintage to compare and contrast with.

Expect to spend at least an hour if not longer learning about the wine making process and tasting the wines. These are not wines you want to rush through. The length of the wines are extravagant and the tastes are exceptional. If you are new to tasting anything remotely close to a Bordeaux, you're in for a treat or a shock, depending upon your palate. The wines are earthy, filled with terrior (not literally, don't worry) and at times feature a smoky characteristic. As one of the wine educators described these wines, "When Bordeaux fans try these wines, their eyes light up."

With big wines come higher prices. The Archipel comes in at $40 and the three wines from Vérité command $150. While the Archipel (still a Bordeaux blend) could be opened now through another 10 years, you're going to want to wait to open up any of the newer Vérité's for a number of years so do consider how your storage situation is at home. Remember that wines dislike three things: movement, sunlight or swift temperature swings.

Remember to plan ahead for this winery. Depending on the time of year, appointments could be difficult to get. And also remember to give yourself some time to get there. Vérité is truly out on its own, both on the caliber of wines and location.

Wine Clubs

It seems that with every tasting room, a wine club awaits you. Some have multi-tiered pricing, some have choice by varietal (usually reds and/or whites), bi-monthly, bi-annually, pick-up, ship it, the choices can be endless. So the question is, is the wine club worth it?

There are pros and cons to signing up for a wine club. Here are a list of a few of them to consider before handing the plastic over.

Pro #1: Every month or two, a few bottles show up in your hands

If you like the winery and the overall taste of the wine is good, getting a few bottles regularly can be quite a treat. For causal wine drinking, two to four bottles every cycle is perfect. Wineries usually give you the option of either shipping it or holding the bottles at the winery.

If the wine club you signed up with is monthly and you elected to pick up the wine yourself, the winery will bunch your orders if more than a month goes by, enabling you the flexibility of not having to drive up every month for a shipment but still reaping the benefits of a monthly service.

Pro #2: Free tastings for you and others

Most all wine clubs waive the tasting fee if you want to taste at the winery in the future. Furthermore, they usually will accommodate your party as well (be sure to check the exact number of guests, as that depends on the individual winery). While it is a small benefit, it is one not to be overlooked.

Pro #3: Access to "reserves" or limited production wines

Sometimes wineries will hold the purchase of limited produced wine to only wine club members. With smaller wineries, they might not even have some wines on the list, so if you decide to join, be sure to ask the winery if they have any "other" wines that might not be poured to the general public. This is one of the biggest reasons for joining a wine club.

Pro #3: Discounts on wine purchases

This is more of a sliding scale, depending on the winery and the tier your membership is at. Most wineries have a flat rate of around 10 to 20% off. As always, be sure to check the winery you are interested in purchasing from. In addition to the general discount, some wineries have multi-tier memberships. That means the more bottles you buy, the bigger the discount.

If you are a big consumer of wine and you love the winery, this can add up to hundreds of dollars saved over the course of the membership. Usually the discount applies to online purchases as well so you don't even have to go to the winery to reap the discounts.

Pro #4: You're the first to get the new releases

I love this one. By getting the wine very soon after it's been bottled, you get the chance to taste how it ages from the very beginning. I've received wine almost a month after it was bottled and the tannins were more rambunctious than Yosemite Sam.

However, about two years later, the tannins mellowed out and the wine was divine. The winery will generally tell you how its going to age, so you can get an idea of how long to cellar it.

Also, a winery will sometimes hold back the release of a wine for awhile to the public, only allowing members to taste and buy it. With some wineries making caseloads of 100 to 200, this is quite a treat, especially if you want to stock up on a certain wine.

Pro #5: Parties!

Wineries know how to throw parties. And of course, they know how to pair the wine and food perfectly. As part of your membership, you're invited to private parties and wine release events. This is a great place to meet fellow wine club members. Depending on the size of the winery, events could come as often as every few months. If curious, ask the person pouring about past events and how often they have them.

Con #1: It can get expensive— quickly

Some wineries ship wine as quickly as every month or two. And if you signed up for a half case, pretty soon you'll have more bottles than your local liquor store. If you elected to ship the wine over picking it up, the shipping costs can rack up quickly. The high costs can quickly sour the taste of the wine.

Con #2: It's only one winery

This is probably the biggest reason why I haven't joined more wineries' wine clubs. While you might like the wine for a month or two, the wines can become repetitious and boring. If the winery only produces three or four wines, and you signed up for a few bottles every other month, there are only so many combinations a winery can put in a shipment. The excitement of a new wine in the mail can quickly wane if you always have a case of the same in the cellar.

Con #3: A Year commitment

Now this doesn't apply to all wineries, but it applies to enough of them to be worth mentioning. Some wineries require a commitment for at least a year from you. That means, even if you are tired of the wine or can't afford the price of the shipment after six months, you're still tied in with them. For all of you out there who curse your cell phone company for their obnoxious contracts, be aware that this is not that far away.

Once again, just read the fine print on the membership. For the ones that don't require this, they usually say that you, "can cancel anytime" or "no commitments." Some of them list this as the first benefit so it is clear you are not locked in.

Wine clubs can be a blessing as well as a curse, depending on whether the club you join fits in with your lifestyle. The euphoria of a membership can quickly wane if it is more of a burden than a welcome treat. I'd recommend going over the options with the person pouring if you are seriously thinking about joining.

About The Author

A native of San Diego, Haydn Adams moved to the Bay Area to attend the Academy of Art University (where he is now a part-time instructor). Armed with a bachelor's of fine arts and one heck of a wine palate, Haydn roams tasting rooms looking for that undiscovered gem of a wine that he is all too happy to share with friends.

As one of his colleagues pointed out, "Haydn's palate is superb and has been reported to taste bottle shock, minute tannins and subtle hints of baked blueberries in wines with one sip." His knowledge of travel further makes Haydn an up-and-coming authority in the wine and travel industries.

In addition to a strict regiment of weekly wine tasting, Haydn also owns and operates his own graphic design company, Nautilus Designs (www.nautilusdesigns.com). He has worked in the graphic design business for well over a decade and has been a pioneer in many graphic design related fields, including Flash design, CD-Rom design and digital video.

Haydn is a member of ZAP, the Zinfandel Advocates and Producers, along with the Graphic Artists Guild. When he's not in the wine country, Haydn can be found on one of the many hiking trails in Marin County, playing trivia and throwing darts at the local pubs and attempting to strengthen his core with Pilates.

Have Palate, Will Travel

Do you know of a winery that you feel is worthy of the title "hidden gem"? If you do, I've love to know about it. I'd love to visit the winery and possibly include the them in future e-newsletters and/or upcoming books. While I'm located in Northern California, I'm always up for a trip to the far side of the world for a mouth-watering Pinot Noir or Tempranillo.

beyondnapavalley.com

For more information on new "hidden gems", to find out where Haydn will be speaking next and to sign up for his e-newsletter, and more.

"Wine is a journey, not a destination, which means that all of us, no matter how much we know, are on the same road, just at different mile markers. If we ever felt we knew everything about wine, we'd move on to stamp collecting—OK, not stamp collecting, but some other hobby. To us, one of the most thrilling aspects of wine is discovering something new to our experience...

...don't make wine into an intellectual exercise. Just enjoy it. Taste, taste, taste. The only way to really know anything about wine is to drink it."

– Dorothy J Gaiter & John Brecher, Wall Street Journal

Beyond Napa Valley
Marin County, California

www.beyondnapavalley.com